After the sudden death of her father, Kasie became an unintentional author. She wanted to create a bond between her then twelve-week-old daughter, Quinn and her father, affectionately known as Poppy. She penned a poem that has since been transformed into a short story to help children hold the memory of their loved ones despite their physical absence.

Grandma Is Now in Heaven

Kasie Kennedy

Austin Macauley Publishers
LONDON • CAMBRIDGE • NEW YORK • SHARJAH

Copyright © Kasie Kennedy 2023

The right of **Kasie Kennedy** to be identified as author of this work has been asserted by the author in accordance with sections 77 and 78 of the Copyright, Designs and Patents Act 1988.

All rights reserved. No part of this publication may be reproduced, stored in a retrieval system, or transmitted in any form or by any means, electronic, mechanical, photocopying, recording, or otherwise, without the prior permission of the publishers.

Any person who commits any unauthorised act in relation to this publication may be liable to criminal prosecution and civil claims for damages.

A CIP catalogue record for this title is available from the British Library.

ISBN 9781398491342 (Paperback)
ISBN 9781398491359 (ePub e-book)

www.austinmacauley.com

First Published 2023
Austin Macauley Publishers Ltd®
1 Canada Square
Canary Wharf
London
E14 5AA

To Ryan, Quinn and Cooper.
Thank you for making sure I never lose my happy.
I love you.

Special thanks to our everyday angels, Gramzi, Mimi &
Papa, Gertie and Mamaw Donna.

Grandma is now in heaven,
But she wants you to know.

She watches over
Wherever you may go.

She checks on you in the mornings,
As your eyes open wide for a new day.

She laughs loudly as she watches
While you smile, giggle and play.

She is there if you may stumble,
When you are feeling down
or blue.

She will be by your side
For the good and bad times, too.

She gathers angels proudly
To look down at you below.

She smiles with love like grandmothers do
As you learn and as you grow.

And when you close your eyes
to pray
Each night as you get ready
for bed,

She whispers a heavenly
"I love you"
As she lays an angel's kiss on your head.